CLYDE ROBERT BULLA

A GRAIN OF WHEAT

A Writer Begins

{ *David R. Godine* • *Publisher* • Boston }

First hardcover edition published in 1985,
first softcover edition in 1988 by
David R. Godine, Publisher, Inc.
Horticultural Hall, 300 Massachusetts Avenue
Boston, Massachusetts 02115

Library of Congress Cataloging in Publication Data

Bulla, Clyde Robert
A grain of wheat

Summary • The author describes his early years,
up until the age of ten, growing up on a Missouri
farm and how he decided to be a writer.
1. Bulla, Clyde Robert—Biography—Youth—Juvenile
literature.   2. Authors, American—20th century—
Biography—Juvenile literature.   3. Farm life—Missouri
—Juvenile literature.   [1. Bulla, Clyde Robert.
2. Authors, American]   I. Title.
PS3503.U544Z463   1985   818'.5403 [B] [92]   84-48750
ISBN 0-87923-568-3 (hc)
ISBN 0-87923-717-1 (sc)

Third printing, November 1991
Printed in the United States of America

To *Glenn, Louise, and Corrine*

A GRAIN OF WHEAT

A Writer Begins

1

The other day a young friend asked me, "Are you going to write another book?"

"I think so," I said. "I hope so."

"What is it going to be about?" she asked.

"I'm not sure yet," I said. "Do you have an idea for me?"

"Yes," she said. "Write a book about yourself."

"Like an autobiography?" I asked.

"Yes, like an autobiography," she said.

"I don't know," I said. "I've lived a long time. If I told about all my life, the book might be too long."

"Well," she said, "couldn't you just tell about *some* of your life?"

I thought that over. The more I thought it over, the more I liked the idea. The book needn't be about *all* my life. I could write about the time I remembered best— the years when I was a boy. And maybe those were the most important years.

So here is another book—a book about some of my life.

I was born on a farm near King City, Missouri, on January 9, 1914. Besides my mother and father, I had two sisters and a brother. My sisters were Louise and Corrine. My brother was Glenn.

Corrine used to tell me, "The rest of us

had good times together when we were growing up. You came along so late you missed all the fun."

I don't think I missed it all. She and my brother pulled me in a cart. That was fun. Neighbors came to our house, and my father played the fiddle while Louise or Corrine played the piano. That was fun, too.

The farmers worked all week and went to town on Saturday night. They went to buy things they needed. At the same time they met their friends. I liked riding to King City in the carriage pulled by our two horses, Mike and Tony. I was five years old before we had a car.

My grandma and grandpa lived in town.

We always stopped at their house. I could look out their kitchen door and see the trains come in.

I didn't know until later that King City was a town. I thought it was a great city. On Saturday night the main street was crowded with people. I had my first nickel bag of candy there, and my first ice cream cone. (I bit off the end of the cone, and the ice cream ran down my shirt.) I saw my first movie there, but I can't remember what it was. It was probably a cowboy picture.

There were interesting things to see and do in town, but I was soon ready to go home. It seemed to me that was where I belonged. I liked our house with its little rooms—two upstairs and three down. My father told me it was almost a hundred years old.

In the back yard were trees—peach, cherry, pear, and black walnut. The vegetable garden was there, too. And there were hollyhocks. Hundreds of them came up and bloomed every spring, with bees buzzing among them.

A few steps from the back door was the well where we let down a wooden bucket and drew up water. It was good drinking water, fresh and clear and cold.

Once the well-rope broke. My father had to climb down to bring up the bucket.

While he was down there, I became very thirsty. We drank from a tin dipper that hung in the kitchen. I took the dipper out to the well and waited. My father was a long time coming up. I looked to see what he was doing, and I dropped the dipper. It hit my father on the head.

He was angry when he came up, and he scolded me.

In the front yard were four mulberry trees, an evergreen, and a big box elder. I used to climb the mulberry trees, and I had a swing in the box elder.

Our front porch faced west. I could sit there and see the barn lot with the big barn and small sheds. I could see the pasture and the woods. Beyond the woods I could see Will Sutton's little brown house half a mile away.

My dog Carlo would be with me on the porch. He was a collie. He was the family dog before I was born, but as soon as I was old enough to play outside he became my dog.

Most of our storms came out of the west. I liked to sit on the porch and watch them. The sky would turn dark, almost black. Lightning would split the clouds, and thunder would crash. Wind would blow and bend the trees, and I would see the rain like a gray curtain falling over the woods. It would sweep across the barn lot and onto the porch, onto my dog and me.

Carlo was afraid of storms. He would shiver and push against me. I remember the smell of his wet fur. I would put my arms around him and we would sit there until my mother opened the door and found us.

"You'll be *soaked*!" she would say and

drag me into the kitchen. But Carlo would have to stay outside. He was never a house-dog.

As I grew older, I played farther and farther from the house. I explored the barn lot, then the pastures, then the woods.

The war came. Everyone talked about the fighting in France. I learned to sing war songs. Someone taught me to march. I marched like a soldier back and forth across the rug with the red roses on it.

My sister Louise made candy and cookies and sent them to a soldier in France. I thought he was lucky, having those good things to eat. She wrote him letters, too. Later he came back and married her and took her away.

3

My mother didn't worry about me as long as Carlo and I were together. She didn't know about the dangerous game we played.

We chased the horses in the pasture. I

waved a stick, and Carlo barked at their heels.

One day I ran too close behind them. One of them kicked me.

Corrine found me in the pasture. I was covered with blood, and the mark of a horse's hoof was on my forehead.

For weeks I lay in bed.

Later my mother told me, "It was a terrible time for us all. We didn't think you would live. Even the doctor didn't think so. You didn't know any of us. You talked without knowing what you were saying. Once you said, 'Too much purple.'"

But I began to get well. I sat up in bed. My mother cut out maps and made me a geography book. I kept it for a long time.

I had forgotten how to walk. I had forgotten how to dress myself and tie my shoes. I had to learn those things all over again.

The doctor took my bandage off and said, "There, he's as good as new."

And I was, except for the scar on my forehead. I still have the scar.

That year my family gave me a special Christmas. I had a Christmas tree. I don't remember how it was decorated—probably with tinsel and crepe paper and strings of popcorn. I do remember that it was beautiful.

Just having the tree would have been enough, but on Christmas morning there were presents! There was a drum. There was a box of candles—red, white, and green. There was a little wooden wagon filled with blocks. There were three books—*Mother Goose*, *Peter Rabbit*, and an ABC book. There was candy, too, and there were popcorn balls and an orange.

Corrine told me Santa Claus had been there in the night.

Just after Christmas there was a snowstorm. The pastures and fields were white, and I was safe and warm inside. I was there with my family. I had my presents. I had my tree.

My mother wanted to take the tree down.

I begged for it to be left up. "One more day," I would say. "Just one more day."

New Year's came and went. My tree was still up.

I had seen a picture of a Christmas tree with candles on it. One day I lighted a candle and tried to set it on my tree.

There was a *whoosh!* like an explosion. The tree burst into flames.

My father picked it up and threw it out into the snow.

I ran into the kitchen. Under the sink was a kind of closet with a small door in it. It was where we kept things we weren't quite ready to throw away— mostly old shoes. I crawled under the sink and shut the door. I lay there in the dark on top of the shoes and I cried. It seems I cried all day.

It wasn't just that my tree was gone. The whole house might have burned.

No one told me to come out from under

the sink. No one scolded me when I did come out. My family must have thought I had been punished enough. For weeks afterward there was a burned spot on the ceiling to remind me of the terrible thing I had done.

4

The three Christmas books were read to me until I knew them by heart. From the ABC book I learned the letters—"A is an apple pie, B bit it, C cut it," and all the rest. From *Mother Goose* I learned about verses and rhymes. And *Peter Rab-*

bit was a good story with good pictures.

I held the books in front of me and pretended to read. I made pencil marks in a tablet and pretended I was writing.

My mother taught me to write *Clyde*.

"Now when you go to school, you'll know how to write your name," she said.

I wanted to read and write, but I didn't want to go to school. Someone had told me tales of what went on at school. They must have frightened me.

Those were the days of country schools. Ours was the Bray School. My sister Louise had taught there before she was married. My sister Corrine had just finished high school and was ready to take Louise's place.

Corrine was teaching for the first time.

I was going to school for the first time.

It was a two-mile walk to school. We started off together. Almost always it rained on the first day of school, but this was a sunny September day. I had my new dinner bucket. There was a beef sandwich in it, and a boiled egg and a banana and a piece of cake. But that gave me no joy.

I said, "I know I'll get a whipping."

"I'll be the teacher," Corrine said. "*I'm* not going to whip you."

Later we learned to cut across pastures and through woods to make the way shorter. On this day we took the road. Past Otis King's, past John King's and Mag Elliott's, over the iron bridge and up the clay hill, past George Haynes's, and there was the school lane.

On one side of the lane was a pasture. On the other side was a row of hedge trees. An odd kind of fruit grew on them. Hedgeballs, we called them. They looked like big green oranges and were good for nothing except to throw at fence posts or roll down hills.

At the end of the lane was the schoolyard, with the schoolhouse in the middle. The schoolhouse was white with a red-brick chimney. It had only one room. The blackboard was up front, along with the teacher's desk and the library. The library was a tall green cupboard with a door.

There were rows of seats and desks for the boys and girls. In the back of the room was a big iron stove.

Corrine and I were the first ones there.

She wrote *Welcome* on the blackboard. Boys and girls began to come from the farms in the neighborhood. There were nine boys and nine girls. Two or three rode horses to school, but most of them walked.

I was in the first grade with three other boys—Leonard, Lawrence, and Harold. Later Lawrence and Harold moved away, but Leonard and I were in school together for years.

When we were called up for our first class, we sat on a long bench in front of the teacher's desk. The teacher asked a question. What would we buy if we had a hundred dollars? I've forgotten what Lawrence and Harold answered. Leonard said he would buy a horse. That was a good answer for a farm boy. I said I would buy a table.

The older boys and girls had been listening. They all laughed at my answer.

Corrine said, "Why would you buy a *table?*"

I said I didn't know.

On the playground, girls and boys said, "A table—a table! What are you going to do with your table?"

And I knew I must guard against saying stupid things.

Still, I liked school. I was surprised at how much I liked it, although I was sometimes sorry my dog couldn't be there. Every day he started off with me. Every day I had to send him back.

5

It took our whole school to make two baseball teams. Besides baseball, we played ante-over, kick-the-can, dare-base, and Indian. In winter we played fox-and-geese in the snow.

George Haynes's pond was near the

school. It was a good place to skate when the ice was smooth and thick enough. Our skates were the kind that clamped onto our shoes. The clamps fastened with a key, and I could never get mine tight enough. My skates kept coming off.

When there was snow, we brought our sleds to school. Each sled had a name. Mine was "The Flying Arrow." Wayne King, who lived across the road from me, had one named "King of the Hills." Coasting down a hill was like flying. Not so much fun was the walk back up, dragging our sleds behind us.

Once during every school-year the boys made what we called a hut. It was a lean-to against the side of the coal-house. We made it of boards, logs—whatever we could find. Tall grass grew under the hedge trees. It dried stringy and tough. We pulled it up until we had a big stack, then we covered the outside of the hut with it. The idea was to cover the hut until it was completely dark inside.

The hut was for boys only. We told the girls they couldn't come in. I can't remember that any of them ever wanted to.

In first grade we had spelling, numbers, reading, and writing. I was slow at numbers, better at spelling. What I really liked were reading and writing. I wanted to learn new words. I wanted to write them and put them together to see what I could make them say.

I would write *apple*. It could be "*an*

apple" or "the apple." It could be on a tree or in a dish. It could be green, red, or yellow.

Words were wonderful. By writing them and putting them together, I could make them say whatever I wanted them to say. It was a kind of magic.

Reading was a kind of magic, too. In a book I could meet other people and know what they were doing and feeling and thinking. From a book I could learn about life in other places. Or I could learn everyday things like tying a knot or building a birdhouse.

By the time I was ready for the third grade, I had read most of the books in our school library. There weren't many. I wanted more. Except for my three Christmas books, we had no children's books at home. I began reading whatever I could find in the family bookcase.

There was a thick book called *Oliver Twist*. It had words I didn't know, but there were many I *did* know, and I was able to read the story all the way through.

Lee, the soldier who married my sister, went to California. Louise followed him, but for a time she was in Missouri while he was far away by the Pacific Ocean. I wrote this poem about them:

California and Missouri

Hand in hand,
Over the sand,
Down by the sea,
And there sits Lee.
'Tis California.

Go out and romp
In the swamp
And pick some peas.
There sits Louise.
'Tis Missouri.

It was my first poem.

I started to write a story, but it was never finished. I called it "How Planets Were Born." This is the way it began: "One night old Mother Moon had a million babies. . . ."

Now I knew why I had said, in the first grade, that I wanted a table. Even then I wanted to be a writer. And didn't writers sit at tables or desks when they wrote?

6

All winter the trees were bare. Winters were so long I was afraid I might forget the leaves—how big they were, what shape, what color. One summer I picked all the different kinds of leaves I could find and pressed them in the big dictionary.

When winter came I took them out, so there was no chance of my forgetting.

Leaves were important to me. Trees were important. I must have known every tree on our farm. One of my favorites was the sycamore that grew by the creek. It was the only sycamore in our woods. Its trunk was smooth—pale brown and silver.

One spring day Sam Reed came to our house. He was our neighbor on the north.

"Get an ax! Get some buckets!" he shouted, and he and my father ran off into the woods.

They came back with the buckets full of honey.

"Where did you get it?" asked my mother.

"From a bee-tree," said my father.

A bee-tree was a tree with a hollow in it where bees had made honey.

"Sam found it," my father said. "He saw bees coming out of a hole in the sycamore tree. We cut it down, and—"

"You cut it down?" I said.

"We had to, to get the honey," he said.

"You cut down the sycamore tree," I shouted, "just for some old honey!"

I went to the woods. I told myself, It isn't true!

But it was. I could hardly bear to look at the sycamore tree lying on the ground.

For a while I wouldn't speak to my father, and I wouldn't eat any of the honey.

I remember that well. I remember this, too.

I said I wished I knew how to swim. My father went to his workshop and came out with two boards. He had nailed them together in the shape of a T.

"Come on," he said.

"Now?" I asked, because the sky was growing dark, and I could see it was going to rain.

"Now," he said.

I went with him through our woods and into the woods across the road. The creek was wider there, with pools big enough to fish or swim in.

We stopped at one of them. I took off my clothes. He floated the T of wood on the water.

"Lie down on it," he said.

I did, and it held me up.

"Paddle," he said.

I paddled and kicked until I was in the middle of the pool. Then I saw that the wooden T had floated out from under me. I was swimming without it.

"Keep going," said my father.

I kept going, across the pool and back. I could swim!

We walked home. Just as we got into the house, there was a crash of thunder, and rain began to pour. I wondered about my father. How had he known how long it would take to walk to the creek, teach me to swim, and walk back before it started to rain?

7

There was always work to be done on a farm. Boys and girls had their special chores. My first ones were filling the woodbox and feeding the animals.

The woodpile was in the barn lot. There were big pieces of wood to be burned in the heating stove. Smaller pieces were for the cook-stove.

Sometimes I carried the wood in my arms. Sometimes I hauled it in a little wagon or the two-wheeled cart. I brought it to the back door and piled it in the woodbox in the kitchen.

I took corn to the pigs and chickens. I fed skim milk to the calves.

In summer I hoed weeds out of the vegetable garden and sometimes out of the cornfield.

But there was time to play, time for long walks in the woods. I looked for rocks along the creek. I knew where to find May apples. They grew on plants that looked like little green umbrellas. The apples were yellow and squashy. They smelled better than they tasted. Ripe gooseberries were good. (Not green ones—they were so sour I could never eat one without making a face.) Wild blackberries were even better. Wild raspberries were best of all.

Always my dog was with me in the woods, until one day. He wasn't waiting when I went out in the morning. He wasn't there when I came back.

Days and weeks went by. I looked for him. I called him. Every evening I went out to the front gate and called, "Here, Carlo—here Carlo!" He didn't come home.

School started. I was in the third grade. Wayne King was in the fifth. He came up to me in the schoolyard. "I know what happened to your dog," he said.

"What?" I asked.

"He's dead," said Wayne. He was look-ing at me, as if he wanted to see how I was taking it.

"He's not dead," I said.

"Yes, he is," said Wayne. "He got poi-soned."

I went home. "Wayne says Carlo is dead," I said.

My father and mother looked at each other.

My mother said, "Yes, he is dead. We didn't want to tell you." Dogs had been killing George Haynes's sheep, she said. He had put out poison for the dogs, and Carlo had eaten some of it.

"George was sorry," my mother said. "He knew how much you liked Carlo."

"Carlo didn't run with other dogs," I said. "Carlo didn't kill his sheep."

"George never thought he did," said my mother. "Carlo just happened to be at his place and ate some of the poison."

She was looking at me, a little the way Wayne had. She must have thought I was going to cry.

I didn't cry. But I missed Carlo. Sometimes I still miss him.

8

As I grew older, I began to see that my mother and father were not happy. It was partly because we were poor, but there were other reasons.

My mother had been a town girl. She had gone through high school. That was more education than most people had in those days. She had never wanted to live on a farm. She thought she belonged in town or in a city.

She wanted to do her work in the morning then put on a pretty dress, sit on the porch, and watch the people go by.

Our house was far back off the road, behind a row of hedge trees. She wanted the trees cut so she could see the road.

My father and brother cut the hedge, but it didn't seem to help. Not many people went by.

My father had more education than my mother. He had gone to college to study science and engineering. He wanted to be the first man to fly. In his father's barn he had started to build an airplane.

His father always laughed at him. "Nobody ever made a plane that would fly," he said. "What makes you think *you* can?"

My Grandfather Bulla had two farms. My father went to work on one of them. That was where he took my mother when they were married.

"We won't stay here long," he said. "This is just till I get into something else."

Years later they were still there.

The Wright Brothers were about my father's age. They made an airplane that would fly.

My father was never the same after he heard about it.

It seemed that he and my mother had

taken a wrong turn. That turn had led them to the farm. Neither of them wanted to be there, but somehow they couldn't get away. I hoped this would never happen to me.

I wanted to be a writer. I was sure of that.

"I'm going to write books," I said.

My mother said, "Castles in the air."

"What does that mean?" I asked.

"It means you're having daydreams," she said. "You'll dream of doing a lot of different things, but you probably won't do any of them. As you get older, you'll change."

I went from the second grade to the third to the fourth, and I hadn't changed. I still knew what I wanted to be.

I thought about writing and talked about it. I talked too much.

My father told me he was tired of listening to me.

"You can't be a writer," he said. "What do you know about people? What have you ever done? You don't have anything to write about."

When I thought over what he had said, it seemed to me he was right. I stopped writing. But not for long.

The city nearest us was St. Joseph, Missouri. Our newspaper came from there. In the paper I read about a contest for boys and girls—"Write the story of a grain of wheat in five hundred words or less." First prize was a hundred dollars. There were five second prizes of twenty dollars each. After that there were one hundred prizes of one dollar each.

I began to write my story. It went something like this: "I am a grain of wheat. I grew in a field where the sun shone and the rain fell."

I didn't tell anyone what I was doing. When my story was finished, I made a neat copy. I mailed it in our mailbox down the road.

10

Time went by. I began to look for the newspaper that would tell who had won the contest. At last it came.

There was a whole page about the contest. I saw I hadn't won the first prize. I hadn't won a second prize either. That was a disappointment. I had thought I might win one of the second prizes.

I read down the long list at the bottom of the page—the names and addresses of the boys and girls who had won the one-dollar prizes. Surely my name would be there. It *had* to be!

I read more and more slowly. Only a few names were left.

And one of them was mine! "Clyde Bulla, King City, Missouri."

"I won!" I shouted.

My mother looked at my name. "That's nice," she said.

Nice? Was that all she could say?

I started to show the paper to my father. There was something in his face that stopped me. I could see he wasn't happy that I had won a prize.

My sister Corrine was there. I could see she wasn't happy either. She was sorry for me because all I had won was a dollar.

Didn't they know it wasn't the dollar that mattered?

I had written a story that was all mine. No one had helped me. I had sent it off by myself. How many other boys and girls had sent their stories? Maybe a thousand or more. But my story had won a prize, and my name was here in the paper. I was a writer. No matter what anyone else might say, I was a writer.